A Friend for Kate

Tony Bradman

Illustrated by Priscilla Lamont

CAMBRIDGE
UNIVERSITY PRESS

Miss Miller was taking Class 1 on an outing
to a farm.

Kate couldn't wait to be Jodie's partner for
the day. Kate and Jodie were best friends.
At least, Kate *thought* they were.

But when the coach arrived at the gate,
Jodie didn't line up with Kate. She lined
up with Laura instead.

Everyone else soon found a partner. Only
Kate was left, standing all alone.

"Never mind, Kate," said Miss Miller.
"You can sit with me. I'll be your
partner today."

The coach set off, and Kate looked
through the window. Jodie and Laura were
sitting behind her.

It took ages to get to the farm. The journey
was boring, and some of the children were
naughty.

"Don't do that, Neal," said Miss Miller.
Jodie and Laura wriggled and giggled.

They reached the farm at last. Everyone
got off the coach, and Miss Miller told them
what to do.

Some of the children couldn't wait to start.
Kate watched Jodie and Laura skip away.

Kate and Miss Miller ticked off
the animals on their list.
They saw the horses,

the cows, the goats, the sheep in their pens,
and the hens.

Kate almost forgot about Jodie.

Then Miss Miller saw some
children being naughty.

"Wait here, Kate," she said. "I'd better
go and sort them out."

Now Kate was all alone again.

But she didn't cry. She had the list, and there was one kind of animal that she hadn't ticked off yet.

It was the kind with a curly tail, the kind
that lives in a sty.

And Kate could hear some of them nearby.

Kate looked over the wall. She saw
a big, fat, snorting mother pig with one,
two, three, four, five, six, *seven* piglets.
Six were cuddled up to her . . .

but one was all alone.

The lonely little piglet looked up.

It came over slowly and sniffed Kate's hand.
She stroked the piglet's head. "I know how
you feel," she said. She did, too!

After a while, Kate thought that she
ought to find the others. But when she
walked away from the sty, the lonely little
piglet ran after her!

It just wouldn't leave her alone!

And everywhere that Kate went, the lonely little piglet was sure to follow. Now, all the children in Class 1 wanted to be Kate's partner . . .

. . . *especially* Jodie and Laura!